UNDIVIDED

A BIBLICAL RESPONSE TO WHAT DIVIDES U.S.

UNDIVIDED

A BIBLICAL RESPONSE TO WHAT DIVIDES U.S.

CHARLES CLEMONS

EQUIP PRESS

Colorado Springs

UNDIVIDED

First Edition: 2020
Undivided / Charles Clemons
Paperback ISBN: 978-1-951304-36-2
eBook ISBN: 978-1-951304-37-9

EQUIP PRESS

Colorado Springs

ENDORSEMENTS

In his brief book, *Undivided: A Biblical Response to What Divides U.S.*, Charles Clemons has accomplished just what he set out to do: he has brought the power of the Scriptures to bear on the contentious issues facing our nation today. With careful scholarship and clear reasoning, Clemons makes a case for a theology of justice that can help to eradicate racism and bring healing to our nation through the Gospel of Jesus Christ. Clemons uses real-life examples to describe the personal impact of unbiblical injustice, and he issues a prophetic call for substantive, biblically based changes. He is unafraid to speak bluntly where needed in addressing the challenges of our day (including the Covid-19 pandemic, racial unrest, and the political stalemate we are experiencing as a nation) but never expresses either bitterness or lack of charity toward those who most need to change to become like Christ in these areas. In fact, the unvarying optimism and kindness found within the pages of this work will remain with you after the last page is turned. Highly recommended!

STEVEN JONES, PRESIDENT
Missionary Church

Undivided: A Biblical Response to What Divides U.S. unapologetically calls a spade a spade and condemns the sin of racism for what it is. In an era when this topic is brushed off, politicized, or analyzed through a secular lens, this book provides a refreshing biblically rooted diagnosis, approach, and solution to the pervasive division among American evangelical churches along ethnic lines. The author calls us to ponder anew what it means for man to be a creature made in the image of God and summons believers to fulfill their mandate to represent God's compassion, justice, righteousness, and impartiality. Rather than a topic to be avoided in conversations within Christian circles, it ought to be a platform upon which the power of the gospel to reconcile men with God and with one another is proclaimed. May this book help each reader assess their own heart, repent from any prejudice against his brother or sister in the Lord, and be an instrument in the King's hands as He gathers for Himself people from every tongue and nation!

FALY RAVOAHANGY
Madagascar 3M, Founder – President

Undivided documents very well the need of the Christian to respond to racism as the Lord does. The history of professing Christian men who taught the wrong gospel is sobering. Understanding this history helps us not deny our shortcomings and better love others—loving others without a negative view of the color of skin or ethnic background, but affirming God-given diversity, as the Lord described in Revelation. Racism is not a black and white issue. It is a matter of pride and hate toward a group of people you have decided are valued less than you. In Christ, there will be a beauty of worship from every tribe, tongue, and every nation.

CHRISTOPHER SUE
Chief Financial Officer, Union Rescue Mission

In his book, *Undivided: A Biblical Response to What Divides U.S.*, Charles Clemons confronts one of the toughest issues that America has been facing for several decades— the issue of racism. He understands that what unites us is far greater than what divides us. Using a Biblical perspective and other well-researched resources, he calls the reader to honor the image of God and cultivate Jesus' compassion as opposed to Jonah's compassion. Clemons is a unicorn voice calling the nation to come back to a merciful and righteous God. He believes in a genuine repentance and a radical change that can only happen through Jesus Christ. Once you decide to read this book, you are taking a risk to change the way you think, and I believe that's the will of the Father for our Church and Nation.

REV. FAUSTIN UZABAKILIHO, PhD
Exodus Vision, President and Founder

Dedication

To my mother and father, Cherrie Eleanor Sheppard-Clemons and the late
Rev. Charles Lee Clemons, Sr., who lived and loved in hard places in the
Name of Jesus Christ. To the memory of Dr. Martin Luther King Jr.
and his commitment to love his neighbor and his enemy for the sake of Christ.
His dream lives on.

ACKNOWLEDGMENTS

To Rev. Arthur Burkes, Dr. Robert Cavin, Rev. Dave DeVries, Pastor Chris Fukunaga, Elder Scott Meadows, Pastor TJ Morsey, Pastor Andre Randolph, and Pastor Ron Seidel, thank you for your godly counsel in this process of writing. Thanks to our pastor, David Cummings, for ongoing support. To my Sister and Brother, Michelle Lawson and Dr. Wayne A. Lawson, for your encouragement in this endeavor. A special thanks to Debra Sullivan Ford and Dianna Sullivan, who enriched *Undivided* with the cover design concept. And to Kim Carter and Annette Tachet for your prayers and insights into the content of the book. To my wife, Noralyn Clemons, thank you for listening and praying with me through it all.

FOREWORD

Dennis D. Engbrecht

The recent wave of racial strife in the United States is not new to our country. Four centuries ago, Virginia colonist John Rolfe documented the arrival of a ship in Jamestown with "20 and odd" Africans on board. A century prior, Europeans had begun transporting kidnapped Africans to Caribbean islands and South America as slave labor. For the past four hundred years, America, initially as an English colony and later as an independent country, has had a contentious relationship with its non-white populous, be they slaves and their descendants, indigenous inhabitants, or immigrants from Asia and south of the U.S. border.

A Civil War, focused on slavery resulting in the deaths of an estimated 700,000 Americans, was followed by a century of Jim Crow laws repressing African Americans and exacerbating racial strife. Those who believed that the Civil Rights Movement of the 1950s and '60s ended racial strife in our nation have been awakened to a reality that half a century later, the sin of racism deeply knit in the fabric of American history continues to rear its ugly head as incidents of police brutality evoked protests and riots in the streets of our cities.

With a backdrop of racism and prejudice in contemporary America, Charles Clemons provides biblical insights to addressing this sin, one he describes as "a heresy." Just as our country has been polarized by racial strife, sadly, many Christians remain divided. While much of the Evangelical church served as the impetus for the abolitionist movement in the nineteenth century, to a great degree the twenty-first-century church, especially that of white evangelicalism, has failed to play a significant role in confronting racial strife. White flight has produced de facto segregation, which, in turn, has isolated Americans based on ethnicity and income.

With a brief but insightful examination of specific historical elements, Charles Clemons has provided evangelicals a path to become undivided through a biblical response to racial strife. Clemons begins in the Old Testament with God's creation of man in his own image. Emphasizing that racism defames the image of God, he goes on to identify the unbiblical nature of segregation and church defended laws against interracial marriage.

In Jonah, we see how God deals with a prophet who has deep-seated prejudices, desiring the Lord's destruction of Nineveh rather than its salvation. In Amos, Clemons draws parallels between the Israel of the prophet's day and America today. God remonstrates against the tolerance of injustice proclaiming ". . . let justice roll on like the water, and righteousness like an ever-flowing stream." The same message applies to the twenty-first century evangelical church. To Clemons, this means restoration and reconciliation between believers of different ethnic and cultural backgrounds.

When Clemons shifts his focus to the New Testament to address racial strife, he uses the example of John Baptist's boldness in addressing immorality, an act that costs him his life. The author challenges the contemporary church for capitulating to political ideologies that run counter to those of Scripture. Unlike John the Baptist, the twenty-first-century evangelical church is too frequently guilty of succumbing to the cultural pressures of the society in which we live to the point that our "transformation" looks no different from that of the world in which we live.

Clemons ends his treatise with a glance at the "kingdom rule of Christ" as revealed in the book of Revelations. The Apostle John's description of heavenly worship around God's throne involving "every tribe and tongue and people and nation" differs drastically from that of the contemporary American church in which eleven o'clock Sunday morning remains the most segregated hour in our nation.

By saturating his work deeply in Scripture, Charles Clemons has provided a path of understanding for racial healing in the twenty-first-century evangelical church. He also includes questions at the end of each chapter, making *Undivided* a valuable workbook for groups of believers who are serious about learning and becoming a part of racial healing in the contemporary church.

And if racial unity does not happen within the bride of Christ, it is unlikely to authentically take place elsewhere. *Undivided: A Biblical Response to What Divides U.S.* provides insights into bringing racial healing to the American church.

DENNIS D. ENGBRECHT, PHD
Senior Vice President Emeritus
Bethel University

CONTENTS

PREFACE

The year 2018 marked the fiftieth anniversary of the assassination of Rev. Dr. Martin Luther King Jr. As a child, Dr. King was my hero for his willingness to boldly speak the truth while demonstrating the love of God to those who hated him. In memory of his life and legacy, I began to write a biblical response to racism to address what has continued to divide our nation along racial lines. Today, this is even more necessary. Frankly, I am shocked and grieved that the Church cannot agree on this lingering issue that continues to plague our nation. For some, even the mere mention of racism causes further division, and I understand that concern. In discussing this topic, many people have no desire to honor God through Christ and unite people in Him. Yet Jesus Christ prayed in John 17:21 that His people would be "one" even as He and the Father are "One."

In America, we live with the complicated legacy of racism—and many Americans still feel the effects of poor law enforcement, employment, housing, and health care, to name a few. So, like addressing any subject, going to the Bible for answers is always appropriate, and the ultimate answer is found in the person and work of Jesus Christ. I will use biblical terms as often as possible to provide solutions for those who name Jesus Christ as Lord. Evidence from the Bible will be given to unbelievers, so they may know that God has made different peoples and nations and desires them to be saved and to worship Him (Matthew 28:16-20; John 3:16, 4; Ephesians 2,3; Revelations 5:1-10).

This book, *Undivided: A Biblical Response to What Divides U.S.*, will use Scripture to explore subjects that relate to our present-day culture of racism. In Chapter 1, you will read about the implications of both true and false views of the image of God in humanity, and how that affects our existence. In Chapter 2, through a study of the life of Jonah, you will discover how God's compassion is different from ours and the great lesson He taught Jonah concerning the people of Nineveh.

In chapter 3, you will read in the book of Amos (and the prophets) about God's view of justice and righteousness and how both matter to Him. In chapter 4, you will review a section of the Gospel of Luke and understand how John the Baptist preached repentance. Specifically, he taught the need to "bear fruits of repentance" (Luke 3:1-20). Genuine repentance and faith in Jesus Christ must affect how we treat others. And finally, in chapter 5, you will ponder the coming worship of Jesus Christ who is called the Lamb (Revelation 5). He will receive worship from people from every tribe, tongue, and nation eternally.

I will share illustrations and historical references to the American experience to biblically address racism. Through the Scriptures, I plan to build a basis for a healthy response to ethnic strife, prejudice, bias, and partiality so that those who name Jesus Christ as Lord would indeed represent Him well as salt and light in a decaying and dark world (Matthew 5:16). May our Lord Jesus Christ be honored in these efforts. Amen.

1 THE IMAGE OF GOD

His Fingerprints On His Creation

Some years ago, on a TV show called *The Antique Roadshow*, people would line up to bring their household belongings to be inspected by a certified antique collector. Interestingly, sometimes people brought an art piece, a painting, or a piece of pottery sold to them at a high price. But later inspection proved it was an imitation, a "knock-off" of little to no value. On the other hand, someone would have in their attic an old vase or lantern they thought was worthless only to discover that it was actually of great value—a masterpiece, a priceless work of art. In today's moral climate, people hate each other and treat each other horribly based on the color of their skin, ethnic background, culture, gender, and all in between. But every human being has been made by the greatest artist in the world—God Himself.

The sin of racism disregards the worth that God ascribed to His creation. In practice and belief, it is an affront to Him (Proverbs 17:5; Acts 10:15). Racism can be a challenge to define biblically because, in its values and firmly held beliefs, it consists of different parts. Generally, one ethnic group is valued and treated preferentially over another.[1] A fuller definition from Scripture is listed below:

Racism is a denial of the image of God (Genesis 1:26–27) and its implications to someone of another ethnicity. Racism

---

1   John Piper, "Racial Harmony and Interracial Marriage," Desiring God, January 16, 2005, https://www.desiringgod.org/messages/racial-harmony-and-interracial-marriage.

in the church is a contradiction of the visible unity of all believers in Christ (Ephesians 2:11-22, Revelation 5:9, 7:9). Racism inside and outside the church is a contradiction of Jesus' command to love our neighbor as ourselves (Mark 12:31, Luke 10:25-27, esp. 29, 37), and of God's creation of all people in His image (Genesis 1:27, Acts 17:26). So theologically, racism entails a denial of the biblical doctrines of creation, man, the communion of saints, and is disobedience to the moral law. We will not mince words. Racism is not only sin, serious sin, it is heresy.[2]

Heretical teaching associated with racism severely harms how people relate to God and men. Like any false teaching, it is passed from person to person and heart to heart. Each person, their family, and community can reinforce or undermine the truth about God and people. In the American experience, as well as globally, deeply held false beliefs about the character of different peoples have been the justification for evil actions, including genocide (See Appendix B – Genocide Historical Dates).

Because all people are created in God's image, they have dignity, worth, and value (Genesis 1:26). It would be unheard of for a person to go into the Louvre Museum in France and deface the Mona Lisa. In the same way, defaming the image of God in words or physical violence is a sin against God.

The topic of the image of God is found in several places in the Bible (Genesis 1:26-28, 9:6; Ephesians 4:24; Colossians 1:15-17, 3:10; James 3:9-12). The above Scriptures describe how man was uniquely made to reflect God. Unlike birds, cattle, insects, and other forms of life and matter, mankind alone, as both male and female, bears the image of God. God commanded Adam and Eve to be fruitful and multiply, fill the earth and subdue it, and have dominion over it.

In some way, man is like God, yet he is not. From the Genesis account, we can ascertain that just as God rules over His creation, mankind rules

---

2   "Racism," Monergism, 2018, accessed Aug 20, 2020, https://www.monergism.com/topics/social-justice/racism.

over his environment under Him. As image-bearers, man is to fill the earth to make it productive and useful and to represent his God throughout the world. We also learn from this passage that God decided to create and to act based on His will. Man, in His image, is endowed with the capacity for knowledge, feelings, and a will. God is in eternal fellowship among God the Father, God the Son, and God the Holy Spirit—one God in three separate persons, the Triune God. In this way, man reflects his Creator regarding fellowship and relationships with fellow image-bearers. All things made at creation were deemed as good (Genesis 1:31).

God alone was to be the source of knowledge of what is right and wrong (Genesis 2:15-17) and gave Adam and Eve the command "not to eat from the tree of the knowledge of good and evil" (Genesis 2:16). By their disobedience, and ours in them, humanity and creation were plunged into futility (Romans 8:19-25) and, as promised, began to die (1 Corinthians 15:22), yet they still retained His image.

In Genesis 9:6, the image of God was the basis for why men must never commit murder. God gave this solemn warning to Noah after destroying the earth for its wickedness and making a covenant with him (Genesis 6-9). Later in Scripture, another warning is issued about human speech. In James chapter 3:9-12, the tongue is depicted as untamable (compared to animals and a ship rudder). With the tongue "men bless God and yet curse men who are made in His image" (v.9). The Apostle James said that "this ought not to be" (v.10). From these few passages, we see that violent acts, physically or verbally, are an assault on the image of God and, thus, a direct offense to God Himself.

Robert Lewis Dabney (1820-1898), Presbyterian pastor, Bible scholar, and chaplain in the confederate army, was noted for his theological contributions. In some of his writings, he provided rich explanations of Bible doctrine to build faith in Christ. An example is the following quote from *On Secular Education*:

> *Every line of true knowledge must find its completeness as it converges on God, just as every beam of daylight leads the eye to the sun. If religion is excluded from our study, every process of thought will be arrested before it reaches its proper goal. The*

structure of thought must remain a truncated cone, with its proper apex lacking.[3]

Home education is a noble act for godly parents to pursue so that their children would come to faith in Christ and discover His vocation (calling) for their lives. Sadly, Dabney also taught white supremacy and had a faulty view of the image of God, seeing black men and their children as inferior morally, intellectually, and culturally. Though he advocated for Christian parents to be the primary educators of their children—thus able to instruct in morality and piety—he also strongly advocated for the separation of the so-called "races," which was in error because there is only one race (human) based on Genesis 1:26. Dabney taught in *A Defence of Virginia*:

> *It is enough for us to say (what is capable of overwhelming demonstration) that for the African race, such as Providence has made it, and where He has placed it in America, slavery was the righteous, the best, yea, the only tolerable relation.... Our system is represented as oppressive and cruel, appointing different penalties for crimes to the black man and the white man; depriving the slave of the privilege of testifying against a white in a court of justice; subjecting him to frequent and inhuman corporal punishments, and making it a crime for him to exercise the natural right of self-defense, when violently assailed by a white man. The reply is, that the penal code of Virginia was properly made different in the case of the whites and the blacks, because of the lower moral tone of the latter...*[4]

It is interesting for Dabney to note that it was the Providence of God to bring Africans to America. But this doctrine of the care and activity of God over His creation is not an endorsement for human sin.

---

3   Robert Lewis Dabney, *On Secular Education* (Russia: Canon Press, 1996).

4   Robert Lewis Dabney, *A Defense of Virginia: (and Through Her, of the South) in Recent and Pending Contests Against the Sectional Party,* (United States: E.J. Hale, 1867), 25, 220, 352-353.

Dabney justified chattel slavery and the misapplication of the law between men. The prophets (e.g., Amos, Jeremiah, etc.) condemned injustice, idolatry, and immorality. Dabney defects from a biblical perspective on the image of God into a form of evolutionary thought to justify slavery. These kinds of justifications resulted in the unjust treatment of slaves, which included kidnapping, torture, rape, murder, separation of families, and daily humiliation of various kinds.

During this age of evolutionary thought, people believed men's intelligence and character were determined by their skull's shape and size (phrenology). Many believed in a hierarchy of people based on observable skin color or so-called "race" like Dabney—none of which are in Scripture The Bible uses two main categories of men, saved and unsaved (John 3:16-19, Romans 3:23, 6:23; Ephesians 2:1-9). Dabney's comments specifically about the image of God are telling. His comments in *A Defence of Virginia* continue:

> *... But while we believe that 'God made of one blood all nations of men to dwell under the whole heavens,' we know that the African has become, according to a well-known law of natural history, by the manifold influences of the ages, a different, fixed species of the race, separated from the white man by traits bodily, mental, and moral, almost as rigid and permanent as those of genus. Hence the offspring of an amalgamation must be a hybrid race, stamped with all the feebleness of the hybrid, and incapable of the career of civilization and glory as an independent race. And this apparently is the destiny our conquerors have in view. If indeed they can mix the blood of the heroes of Manassas with this vile stream from the fens of Africa, then they will never again have occasion to tremble before the righteous resistance of Virginian freemen; but will have a race supple and vile enough to fill that position of political subjection, which they desire to fix on the South"*[5]

---

5   ibid, 352-353.

Some who are quick to defend Dabney assert that much of his writing honored Christ and the above awful comments reflect a man of his times. Though he wrote Christ-honoring works, we can also learn from his errors and how they have affected others. This may better help discern errors being repeated in our own day, subtly or overtly. Scholars who study the "*imago Dei*" have seen an eerie denial of it within American society and, at times, the complicity of the American church.

One of the founding fathers of America, Thomas Jefferson, penned the words, "We hold these truths to be self-evident: that all men are created equal; that they are endowed by their Creator with certain unalienable rights; that among these are life, liberty, and the pursuit of happiness." In its basic reading, it is a true statement affirming Genesis 1:26-28. Yet Thomas Jefferson owned slaves. Dabney and other Christian slaveholders affirmed the image of God in some men and denied it in others. A contemporary of R. L. Dabney—famed British "prince of preachers" Charles Spurgeon—strongly condemned slavery and had his life threatened because of it. Spurgeon said the following about the violation of the image of God among enslaved Africans:

> *By what means think you were the fetters riveted on the wrist of our friend who sits there, a man like ourselves, though of a black skin? It is the Church of Christ that keeps his brethren under bondage; if it were not for that Church, the system of slavery would go back to the hell from which it sprung…But what does the slaveholder say when you tell him that to hold our fellow creatures in bondage is a sin, and a damnable one, inconsistent with grace? He replies, "I do not believe your slanders; look at the Bishop of So-and-so, or the minister of such-and-such place, is he not a good man, and does not he whine out 'Cursed be Canaan?' Does not he quote Philemon and Onesimus? Does he not go and talk Bible, and tell his slaves that they ought to feel very grateful for being his slaves, for God Almighty made them on purpose that they might enjoy the rare privilege of being cowhided by a Christian master? Don't tell me," he says, "if the thing were wrong, it would not have the Church on its side."*

And so, Christ's free Church, bought with his blood, must bear the shame of cursing Africa, and keeping her sons in bondage.[6]

Spurgeon clearly had in view the *imago Dei*, the commandment to love your neighbor, and the inconsistency of denying the grace of God toward others when it has been received at Christ's expense. Spurgeon was aghast at the contradiction in the life of the church that condoned and participated in slavery. Today, when injustice occurs toward anyone or toward God's honor, Christians should be moved to speak out (Proverbs 31:8, Isaiah 1:17). Though slavery was abolished in the United States, the thinking and heart convictions that started this institution endured.

This false view of the image of God can also be seen in some elements of the homeschooling movement. After the various civil rights acts of the 1950s and 60s, many opposed to school integration began to develop Christian academies and homeschool associations to exclude non-white ethnic groups. The teachings of Rousas J. Rushdoony (1916-2001) had a degree of influence in the homeschool movement. He strongly advocated for the separation of races, as did R. L. Dabney. In *The Biblical Philosophy of History*, Rushdoony states:

> *The white man has behind him centuries of Christian culture, and the discipline and selective breeding this faith requires. Although the white man may reject this faith and subject himself instead to the requirements of humanism, he is still a product of this Christian past. The Negro is a product of a radically different past, and his heredity is governed by a radically different consideration.*[7]

Aspects of this statement are problematic. It assumes that what he considers "white men" and "black men" are monolithic in their spiritual

---

6   Charles Haddon Spurgeon, "Separating the Precious from the Vile," *The New Park Street Pulpit*, vol. 6 (Grand Rapids: Baker, 1994), 155.

7   Rousas Rushdoony, *John. The Biblical Philosophy of History*, (United States, Ross House Books, 2000), 88-89.

states. He presumed that Christian culture was limited to only "white men." Interestingly, Africa (Sudan, Ethiopia) had Christians as early as the late first century (Acts 8:26-40). Churches began to be planted in the Axumite Empire and Ethiopian kingdoms. As Christian traders traveled southward, and even through the salt trade, the gospel began to spread in Africa long before America was colonized.[8]

As Christians are faithful to preach the gospel (Mark 16:5), all peoples will have an opportunity to hear the truth. So-called "selective breeding" will not secure salvation for a man born in Africa, Asia, or Europe. The problem with firmly held beliefs influenced by racism is that they hinder the ability to discern character beyond appearance. When Samuel outwardly evaluated the sons of Jesse to determine the next chosen king of Israel, God corrected him and said, "Man looks on the outward appearance, but God sees the heart (1 Samuel 16:7). In the *Institutes of Biblical Law*, Rushdoony states the following concerning the right of an employer to prefer an employee based on "color, creed, race or national origin":

> *All men are not equal before God; the facts of heaven and hell, election, and reprobation make it clear that they are not equal. Moreover, an employer has a property right to prefer whom he will in terms of "color, creed, race, or national origin." A Japanese Christian church in Los Angeles has the right to call a Japanese Christian pastor. A Swedish or a Negro employer has a right to hire whom he will, in terms of what is most congenial to his purposes.[9]*

In trying to apply the Mosaic law to the U.S. workplace, Rushdoony falls into error in his view of man. All men are equally made in the image

---

8   Elizabeth Isichei, *A History of Christianity in Africa: From Antiquity to the Present.* (United States, Eerdmans Publishing Company, 1995).

9   Rousas John Rushdoony and Gary North, *The Institutes of Biblical Law*, (United States, Presbyterian and Reformed Publishing Company, 1973).

of God (Genesis 1:26). All men fall short of the glory of God due to sin and require grace for salvation (Romans 3:23; Ephesians 2:8-9). He had elevated preferences (i.e., related to hiring practices and culture) to a place of importance. Understandably, various ethnic groups may prefer someone of their background, but the Old and New Testaments affirm godly character as the primary qualifier (Exodus 18:1-27; 1 Timothy 3; and Titus 1).

Pastor John Piper recounted that in 1967, Warren Webster, former missionary to Pakistan, spoke at the Urbana Missions Conference. A student had asked, "What if your daughter falls in love with a Pakistani while you're on the mission field and wants to marry him?" He responded, "The Bible would say, *Better a Christian Pakistani than a godless white American!*"[10] Unlike Webster, firmly held beliefs about different ethnic groups and "breeding" are hints of a form of scientific racism inherent in Darwin's writings (e.g., *Origins of Species*).[11]

This false view of the image of God has considerably shaped American life. As a theology, some have called this Kinism, which is a blending of Christian doctrine with separatist (and disparaging) views concerning immigrants. In "The Kinist Heresy: A Biblical Critique of Racism," Brian Schwertley provides this overview of Kinism:

> …a rapidly growing movement among professing Christians called kinism. Kinist or kinism comes from the word kin, such as "kith and kin." The movement seems to be particularly popular among conservatives and ex-theonomists (I say extheonomists because kinism is essentially racist and antinomian). Its appeal lies in the idea that dark-skinned immigrants to the United States, be they African, Mexican or Caribbean, (generally

---

10   John Piper, "Racial Harmony and Interracial Marriage," Desiring God, January 16, 2020, accessed August 21, 2020, https://www.desiringgod.org/messages/racial-harmony-and-interracial-marriage.

11   Charles Darwin, *On the Origin of Species by Means of Natural Selection, Or, The Preservation of Favoured Races in the Struggle for Life*, (United Kingdom, G. Richards, 1902).

speaking) tended to be socialistic in their outlook, more involved in crimes, and a drag on the United States culturally, politically, and socially.[12]

Elements of this movement were involved in the 2016 #Unite the Right Protest, where men carried tiki torches and chanted the Nazi phrase, "Blood and Soil" – a reference to a German national identity prevailing over any external group seeking to replace them. The young men were heard saying, "You will not replace us!" and "Jews will not replace us!" In response, protesters clashed with them. Many have spoken against what some consider far-left groups, calling out Marxist views and Socialist agendas.

It is greatly concerning that some professing Christians, consumed with a hyper patriotism, have been swept along with a nationalist movement akin to Nazi Germany, with a growing following sympathetic to Adolf Hitler. How much of the present resurgence of ethnic strife can be attributed to such views? Professing Christians can now be heard at political rallies saying, "Go back to your country!" and see no contradiction with the command to love God and your neighbor (Matthew 22:36-40). Christians must challenge these ideas; otherwise, our culture will repeat events such as the Chinese exclusion Act of 1882, the Japanese internment of 1942, or the separation of families at the border of 2018. Therefore, we can conclude that the image of God is being violated (Genesis 9:6; Matthew 5:44; James 3).

Some prominent Bible seminaries historically did not admit African Americans or ethnic minorities well into the 1960s–1970s. Since then, some have publicly renounced their former teaching and have taken steps in keeping with the gospel (Galatians 2,3). Many church covenants and restrictive community covenants employed unbiblical classifications of race and excluded people from church worship, the purchase of homes outside of urban areas, or terrorized individuals found in certain towns

---

12   Brian Schwertley, "The Kinist Heresy: A Biblical Critique of Racism," accessed August 21, 2020, http://www.reformedonline.com/uploads/1/5/0/3/15030584/kinist_heresy.pdf.

after sundown. These are well-documented historical facts, including the use of "the Green Book" by African Americans to avoid falling prey to hostile communities.

Using history to illustrate false views of the image of God is not meant to elicit a false sense of guilt or superiority but to speak the truth and honor Christ. Today, many associate the teachings of Christ with bigotry and not with the good news that God sent His Son into the world to die for our sins and rise again as Lord and Savior of our lives (1 Corinthians 15:3-4). We cannot repent for other's sins, but we can acknowledge their effects upon us or others today and strive not to repeat them (Isaiah 6:5; Ezekiel 18). Also, the subtle normalcy of evil can fool anyone into accepting ghastly things as long as it does not directly affect the individual.

In his article "When Evil has Nice Manners," Trevin Wax described how "normal people" who live next door may be Nazi sympathizers and how evil lurks in all hearts closer than we think. Wax wrote the following:

After having endured the Gulag, Alexander Solzhenitsyn, the Russian dissident, did not come away with the idea that evil is "out there" to be quarantined and set aside in jails and prisons. No, he realized that "the line separating good and evil passes not through states, nor between classes, nor between political parties either—but right through every human heart—and through all human hearts." To be sure, it is unsettling to think that the kind kid down the street could become an ISIS radical, or that the boy who sits behind you in church could be visiting neo-Nazi websites, or that the talkative woman you talk to on the subway aids and abets a man in power who preys on others. Of course, it's unsettling that your next-door neighbor may love Seinfeld, eat cherry pie, and feel fondness for Hitler![13]

The sin of racism at root is an issue of the heart. Like a parasite, as referred to by Wax, this form of evil can exist alongside everyday normal

---

13   Trevin Wax, "When Evil has Nice Manners," The Gospel Coalition, December 11, 2017, https://www.thegospelcoalition.org/blogs/trevin-wax/nazi-next-door-normalcy-evil/.

life. Like any other evil, this sin can only be removed through the power of God, through repentance and faith in Jesus Christ. As the Scripture teaches, "Who the Son sets free, is free indeed" (John 8:36). When racism is found in the church or condoned (e.g., Robert Lewis Dabney and Rousas J Rushdoony, both associated with Kinism presently) by the church, it discredits the Name of Jesus Christ before a watching world.

A false view of the image of God can be traced to most historical genocides (see Appendix B). To be clear, these actions are sin. And as evidenced, they are not limited to the continent of Europe but have occurred in Africa, in Asia, and in the Americas. This is a picture of the depravity of man across the ages, reflective of a darkened heart and conscience (Romans 1-3).

The most prevalent genocide, which regrettably occurs nearly daily in the United States, is abortion. The architect of this movement is Margaret Sanger. Sanger birthed *Planned Parenthood* from a belief in racial superiority, and its natural conclusion was the systemic genocide of unborn inferior races.[14] This has also been called eugenics. Her view of the pseudo-science of eugenics is illustrated in her statement, "*Eugenics is ... the most adequate and thorough avenue to the solution of racial, political and social problems.*"[15] To Sanger, Eugenics was her key to solving societal ills. As a science, eugenics seeks to improve humanity through selective breeding, contraception, and now more prevalently...abortion. The sinister thought is that man is not a product of the Creator but a "thing" to be disposed of if not desired.

Not unlike that belief system held by Adolph Hitler and those in favor of Nazi Germany, eugenics exalts certain "ideal" people and destroys others. In fairness to Margaret Sanger, she often expressed sorrow at the poverty of those living in slums. But her solution morphed into the destruction of those same lives. Historically, Sanger aligned herself with African American leaders and ministers to promote her views of

---

14   M. Sanger, M.W. Perry, and H.G Wells, *The Pivot of Civilization in Historical Perspective: The Birth Control Classic*, (Inkling Books, 2003).

15   Margaret Sanger, "The Eugenic Value of Birth Control Propaganda," *Birth Control Review* (October 1921): 5.

decreasing poverty. The following are her words on what was called "The Negro Project:"

We should hire three or four colored ministers, preferably with social-service backgrounds, and with engaging personalities. The most successful educational approach to the Negro is through a religious appeal. And we do not want word to go out that we want to exterminate the Negro population, and the minister is the man who can straighten out that idea if it ever occurs to any of their more rebellious members.[16]

African American leaders such as W. E. B. Dubois, Mary McCloud Bethune, and former U.S. Representative Adam Clayton Powell Jr.—either knowingly or unknowingly—aligned themselves with Sanger through her educational and award programs even though Sanger viewed African Americans, Southern Europeans, and immigrants as genetically inferior. Her eugenics views were condemned by many for what they were, a call for genocide. But some accepted them, and many abortion clinics are located in urban areas today. Margaret Sanger and the founders/supporters of Planned Parenthood are rooted in unbelief concerning all men made in the image of God (Genesis 1:26, 9:1-6). Eugenics as a science sought to judge the value of men based upon the standard of mankind and not the supreme worth of his Creator.

All people have the privilege of bearing the image of God. The perfect example of the image of God is found in Jesus Christ (Colossians 1:15-17). If you name Him as your Lord and Savior, how you treat people will reflect directly on how they view Him. No other figure of humanity is deserving of exaltation above others except Jesus Christ. Yet Jesus Christ, who existed (and still does) as deity, chose to humble Himself, take on the form of a man, and even die a sacrificial death as a slave (Philippians 2). This is the attitude

---

16   Margaret Sanger, Commenting on the 'Negro Project' in a letter to Dr. Clarence Gamble, December 10, 1939. - Sanger manuscripts, Sophia Smith Collection, Smith College, North Hampton, Massachusetts. Also described in Linda Gordon's *Woman's Body, Woman's Right: A Social History of Birth Control in America.* (New York: Grossman Publishers, 1976).

Christians must have toward all people (Jew, gentile, immigrant, native-born, First Nations, etc.). Sadly, many in America do not view Christians as reflecting Christ. And false teaching concerning the image of God has cultivated an illegitimate sense of exclusion from the world.

Jesus said, "Let your light so shine, so that people would see your good works and glorify your Father in Heaven" (Matthew 5:16). When Christians affirm by their words, deeds, and their faith that all people are truly made in the image of God, they will stand out from ordinary men. Then as Christians, we can relate to all people as being one in Adam via the gospel of Jesus Christ that unites us in Him (Romans 5:12-21; 1 Corinthians 15:22).

PRAYER

"Heavenly Father, in the Name of Jesus Christ. Our times are in Your hands. We thank you for the gift of life. We thank you for the privilege to bear your image in this world. To you alone belong Sovereignty over all nations. Please forgive us for being unloving toward our neighbors, and even our enemies, who also bear your image. Help us to worship and reflect you in spirit, in deed, and in truth, in the Name of Jesus Christ. Amen."

DISCUSSION QUESTIONS

1. What does the Bible say about the image of God (see Genesis 1:26-28, 9:6, James 3)?
2. How often are political views shaped by an understanding of the image of God?
3. What role does the Church play in teaching on the image of God?
4. How does the gospel of Jesus Christ affect the heart concerning the image of God?
5. Can a true Christian remain racist (sinfully prejudiced) for life?
6. In discipleship, how can the image of God be taught?

2 JONAH

God's Compassion Is Different From Ours

Cynics of the Christian faith have said, "I'd rather see a sermon than hear one!" But the Bible teaches that "faith comes by hearing, and hearing by the Word of Christ" (Romans 10:17). Hearing the Scriptures is essential. Yet genuine faith will be demonstrated by good works (Matthew 5:16-17; Ephesians 2:8-10). An outworking of real faith is compassion, which is love in action.

Recently, a six-year-old boy and his little sister were attacked by an unleashed dog, and they feared for their lives. The boy quickly got between the dog and his sister and was mercilessly bitten. Thankfully, he survived and was hailed a hero. The boy risked death in the place of his sister, saying to himself in that moment, "If someone had to die, I thought it should be me." He acted bravely with compassion.

True compassion comes from God. It is sacrificial and reflects and honors Christ. It is otherworldly. It is inspiring, beautiful, and compelling. But the sin of racism is evidenced by a lack of compassion for those deemed inferior. Genuine Christian faith will reveal compassion for the lives of the most vulnerable and defend the cause of the poor (Proverbs 29:7; Matthew 25:31-46; James 1:27). The compassion of Jesus Christ moved Him to feed the poor (Mark 6:34-44), while the lack of compassion by the "rich man" led him to see poor Lazarus daily yet not be moved to help (Luke 16:19-31). The story of Jonah is a picture of hideous compassionless faith. As a prophet whose words are few in Scripture, we learn about Jonah mainly through observing his deeply ingrained prejudice against the Ninevites and his self-serving ways (Jonah 1-4). But outside the book containing his name, a reference is made to him in 2 Kings 14:23-25:

In the fifteenth year of Amaziah son of Joash king of Judah, Jeroboam son of Jehoash king of Israel became king in Samaria, and he reigned forty-one years. He did evil in the eyes of the LORD and did not turn away from any of the sins of Jeroboam son of Nebat, which he had caused Israel to commit. He was the one who restored the boundaries of Israel from Lebo Hamath to the Dead Sea, in accordance with the word of the LORD, the God of Israel, spoken through his servant Jonah son of Amittai, the prophet from Gath Hepher.

Interestingly, God used Jonah to prophesy to the king of Israel that they would regain lands that were lost to surrounding enemies. Yet 2 Kings 14:23-25 describes Jeroboam II as evil and not departing from the sins of his predecessor, King Jeroboam I, who led Israel into idolatry (1 Kings 12:25-33; 14:6-11). Jeroboam I succeeded King Solomon, but he, along with the nation of Israel, marked an increased departure from following the LORD God to idols. By the reign of Jeroboam II, the nation of Israel was plummeting toward spiritual bankruptcy.

Israel had lost lands in the Hamath-Damascus region to their enemies. Under Jeroboam II, they experienced military victories and prospered financially, so all seemed well in Israel. Later, the prophet Amos confronted Israel for their rampant idolatry and immorality (Amos 2:4-16; 5:10-27) and prophesied that the same lands would actually be retaken by invaders (Amos 6:13-14),[17] thus reversing previous gains as punishment.

Israel reflected the spiritual state of their leaders. Jeroboam II pursued material prosperity but neglected true worship and justice at the gate (equitable execution of the law). The "Gate" was the location in Israel where the elders and leaders ruled on the law (Deuteronomy 21:19; Ruth 4:1-12). The attitude of the Israelites was also like their prophet Jonah—self-satisfied, smug, and indifferent toward their relationship with God

---

17   T. Mackie and J. Collins, J. et al., "Bible Overviews: Old Testament: Jonah," The Bible Project, accessed July 2020, https://bibleproject.com/all-videos/read-scripture-old-testament/.

and their neighbor (fellow Israelite, the poor, and the alien). This led to idolatrous, ritualistic worship devoid of true compassion. Enter Jonah into the pages of Scripture.

The rebellious prophet flees from God's commission to *"cry against it, for their wickedness has come up before Me"* (Jonah 1:2). Instead, Jonah flees from the presence of the LORD (v.2) into his downward path from Israel, to Joppa, headed toward Tarshish (vv.1-5), downward into the bowels of a ship where he was asleep. At the start of this little book, many contradictions are present. His name "Jonah" means "dove." And "son of Amittai" means "son of faithfulness." His actions in history were the opposite of dove-like and faithful. As he sleeps during the raging storm, the non-Israelite sailors are crying out to any god that would hear them. Jonah, after having been awakened and questioned as to his occupation and origin, says, "I am a Hebrew, and I fear the LORD God of heaven who made the sea and the dry land" (v.9). This statement is the opposite of Jonah's actions. It is hypocrisy.

The book of Jonah holds a mirror up not only to the Israelite of that day but to us today. Is it possible to be a worshipper of the true and living God and be asleep to the perils of your neighbor or, worse, despise them enough to flee from them when called to have compassion toward others? Before I received Christ Jesus as my Lord and Savior, I worked at a camp for inner-city youth while in college. One summer, I saw a young African American man of fourteen on the street selling drugs. Concerned, I asked him why he was doing this.

The young man said, "My mother is on crack cocaine, and my little brother and I need to eat. Besides, I don't want him to be taken away if the social worker finds out that we don't have food...."

I was speechless. Barely a few years older than him, I begged him not to continue selling and tried to get help for him. To this day, I do not know where he is. As a Christian, when I see the news of a young person shot or arrested for drugs or any crime, I am less judgmental and am moved by compassion to share the love of Christ through the gospel and any meaningful way I can help. Jonah slept while the crew were near death. His sleep was not from an abiding trust in the Sovereign Lord but an imbedded indifference to the woes of his fellow man.

In an act of seeming self-sacrifice, Jonah commands the sailors to throw him overboard so the storm will subside (vv.12-17). Yet the noble sailors plead with God not to punish them for sin in taking the life of Jonah or for any of his sins. The sailors later offer a sacrifice to the LORD (v.16), which indicates that they came to genuine faith in the true and living God.

The LORD ordained a fish to swallow Jonah, thus saving his life, and three days later, after pleading and returning to his vow, he commits to going to Nineveh. After traveling throughout this great city, people great and small, including livestock, repent in sackcloth and ashes. At the sight of their corporate and individual repentance, God relents of the calamity that was to destroy Nineveh (3:10), which greatly displeased Jonah. Jonah 4:1-3 records his complaint toward the LORD God:

> *But it greatly displeased Jonah and he became angry. He prayed to the LORD and said, "Please LORD, was not this what I said while I was still in my own country? Therefore, in order to forestall this, I fled to Tarshish, for I knew that You are a gracious and compassionate God, slow to anger and abundant in lovingkindness, and one who relents concerning calamity. Therefore now, O LORD, please take my life from me, for death is better to me than life.*

Jonah knew who God was theologically, accurately describing His character as "gracious," "compassionate," "slow to anger," and "abundant in lovingkindness." These words are found in Exodus 34:6. Yet Jonah disobeyed the command to love his neighbor (Leviticus 19:18, 34). And Jonah is angry with God because he knew His compassion would spare his enemies, the people of Nineveh. Jonah rebukes God and recalls the reason he did not want to go and leave his own country in the first place. Jonah even pleads that his life would be taken (Jonah 4:3). Amazingly, the Lord God patiently asks Jonah, "Do you have any good reason to be angry?" (v.4).

God, in His wisdom, was patient with Jonah and He is patient today. The Lord God has the right to show compassion and mercy to whomever He will. Jonah did not understand or accept that. He was preoccupied with himself and his possessions, and God would teach Jonah a lesson by using a plant. In this final chapter (Jonah 4), overnight a vine grows and provides shade for Jonah, and that makes him extremely happy. But later God appoints a worm to attack and devour the plant until it withered. Later, God appoints a scorching Sirocco wind to cause him to be faint and weary to the point of death. Again, Jonah begs God to take his life, saying, "Death is better to me than life." And God asks, "Do you have any good reason to be angry about the plant?" (v.9). And Jonah, persisting, answers, "I have good reason to be angry even to death."

Here, God gives the final lesson to Jonah, explaining that he was concerned about the plant, which he did not bring into existence or cause to grow. Should He not have compassion on Nineveh, the great city, which had more than 120,000 people who did not know their right hand from their left? And Jonah provides no answer to the question. This story turns the mirror toward us. We live in a materially wealthy land. Compared to the majority population of the world who lives on less than $2.50 per day,[18] the United States, as well as the West, generally enjoys material prosperity. Yet at times, our actions and attitudes toward immigrants and the poor are often without compassion and, in some cases, with cruelty.

I have a Christian friend who grew up in Iraq and Iran before moving to the United States. He has family in the regions of Nineveh, Iraq who maintain their faith in Jesus Christ. While living in America, it is been hard for him to find a church to actively worship in due to the hostility toward his middle-eastern ethnic background, and many churches fail to clearly teach the Word of God without promoting exalted political allegiances from the pulpit. I know him to be a prayerful, dear man of God who has regularly prayed for my family.

When he was attending a well-known church service, a video played showing terrorists beheading Christians in the middle east. In addition

---

18   Anup Shah, "Poverty Stats and Facts," Global Issues: Social, Political, Economic and Environmental Issues That Affect Us All, accessed September 2020, https://www.globalissues.org/article/26/poverty-facts-and-stats#:~:text=Poverty%20Facts%20and%20Stats%201%20Almost%20half%20the,to%20be%20underweight%20or%20stunted.%20More%20items...%20

to this horrific imagery, a good deal of political rhetoric was shared and the people began to call for war against Iraq. My friend was horrified and pleaded with them to embrace the need to share the gospel because people in these regions love Jesus Christ too. Unfortunately, his pleading fell on deaf ears. Finally, he said, *"I will support you sending bombs over to my homeland if you'll take your children and place them on a plane, fly them over there, and have them be with mine as those bombs are dropped."*

The government bears the sword, ordained by God, yet Christians must strive to live at peace with all men (Romans 12:18, 13:1-4). In examining our hearts toward God and others, is there compassion or do we think more highly of ourselves (individually or corporately, Romans 12) than our neighbor? Is our response like Jonah or is it more like the greater Jonah, who is Jesus Christ?

The Bible says He came to His own and His own did not receive Him, but to those who received Him, to them He gave the right to be children of God, even to those who believe on His Name (John 1:11-12). Jesus Christ is the greater Jonah who was in the grave for three days and later rose again and is seated at the right hand of the Father. He had compassion as He looked out on the multitude of people who looked like sheep without a shepherd (Matthew 9:36). This compassion moved Jesus Christ to act, which led Him to the cross. The cross demonstrated the love of God in action (John 3:16). God, who has not changed, is still compassionate and gracious. The story of Jonah reminds us that God will judge sin (like Nineveh and the U.S.) but is willing to forgive sinners because He is compassionate and gracious. The question remains, are you?

PRAYER

"Our Heavenly Father, thank you for being compassionate, gracious, slow to anger, and abounding in mercy. We desperately need each of these perfections from you every day. Please help us to reflect these toward our neighbors and our enemies so that all may turn to you in genuine repentance and faith in the Name of Jesus Christ. Amen."

DISCUSSION QUESTIONS

1. When discussing issues, do you have compassion toward your opponent? Your enemy?
2. Are there any parallels between the ancient leaders of Israel and leaders today?
3. Can national prosperity become an idol to America and the church? If so, how?
4. How can Christians be compassionate to aliens and immigrants?
5. In the matter of ethnic prejudice, is your attitude more like Jesus Christ or Jonah? Why?

3 AMOS

God Requires Justice And Righteousness

A man who had explosive arguments with his wife later divorced her. As a result of his previous violent actions toward her, he had a restraining order against him. He later became physically ill and was hospitalized due to an incurable disease. At his lowest point, he begged God for another chance, though he felt he did not deserve it. When I visited him, he prayed to the Lord Jesus Christ for forgiveness, fully accepting the likelihood that he would die.

Amazingly, he survived. His health improved. Along with an increased appetite, his weight and stamina returned. This man read the Bible and prayed with a sense of gratitude, humility, and hope. Soon he was discharged from the hospital and knew he would have to return to court to face the consequences of his previous actions. Nearly a year earlier before being hospitalized, he had violated his restraining order and went to see his ex-wife, where another argument occurred. He now recognized that he was wrong and accepted that he would have to pay the consequences. He repented of his sins and was ready to face his sentence and asked me to stand with him during court.

The judge was firm and appeared unyielding in his description of the seriousness of breaking the law. Based upon the evidence, the judge ruled that he would serve a prison sentence of twelve to fourteen months immediately.

As the man was preparing to go to prison, he asked the judge, "May I pray with my pastor before leaving?"

The judge curiously turned and asked, "Do you have a pastor here?" and then turned to me and said, "You! Please come before the court."

With this impromptu meeting, I was asked about the man's character. Specifically, had he changed since I had known him? I was glad to say that he was genuinely sorrowful for his wrongs (2 Corinthians 7:10) and that he was making restitution to people he had hurt. He was restoring property, issuing apologies where able, learning to control his anger according to Scripture, and cultivating peaceful relationships. The judge immediately halted carrying out the prison sentence. To our relief and joy, he ordered the man to do community service through the church.

That day, justice was served. Restorative justice occurred instead of solely retributive justice (punishment). In the Old and the New Testaments, justice and righteousness are taught concerning our relationship with God and our neighbor. The man was humbled in knowing he had broken the law. Due to his new relationship with God through repentance and faith in Christ, he understood what he had done. Justice must be served, yet God in His mercy restored him and used him to restore things that had been broken in his life.

The Bible teaches that righteousness and justice are the foundation of the throne of God (Psalm 89:14). He sets the standard of righteousness and commands what is required ethically, morally, and spiritually among all people. He is just and requires that His people act concretely in ways that bring about justice in the world. As followers of Jesus Christ, we abide under the law of Christ, which is loving your neighbor and loving God with all your being (Mark 12:29-31). This justice is relational.

Justice and mercy are important to God and can be neglected in our relationships with our fellow man. Jesus Christ rebuked the Pharisees for prioritizing their religious observances but failing to treat people justly. Matthew 23:23 reads, "Woe to you, scribes and Pharisees—hypocrites! —because you pay a tenth of mint and dill and cumin and neglect the more important matters of the law—justice and mercy and faithfulness! It was necessary to do these things while not neglecting those." Jesus Christ affirmed that justice, mercy, and faithfulness are "the more important matters of the law."

The Pharisees were known to take extra care in observing Israel's ceremonial laws, yet they often treated their fellow citizens and immigrants of Israel badly. Interestingly, Jesus Christ made clear His view of the Old

Covenant laws, that He did not come to do away with the law but to fulfill it (Matthew 5:17). We can discern from the Scriptures that God takes justice seriously. The justice of God may be retributive to punish sin and restorative to bring us back into a right relationship with Him and with fellow image-bearers. The prophets consistently warned Israel of their injustice.

The prophet Amos was sent by God to warn Israel of the coming judgment upon their idolatry and rampant injustice. Amos was an unusual prophet because he was an ordinary farmer. He was not from the family of a prophet, but he was a fig picker and herdsman (7:14-15). His message of impending judgment was to "those who were at ease in Zion" (6:1,6). They grew comfortable as the chosen people of God and did not perceive their peril. They had a form of self-satisfied religion where they actively wanted the blessing of God for themselves and family yet had little concern for their neighbor. God used Amos to challenge that with imminent justice through certain exile (5:27; 7:11, 43) yet with hope of restoration (Amos 9:11-15).

The book begins in Amos chapters 1 and 2 with a series of judgments on the nations surrounding Israel and her sister nation Judah. Each country is judged for its sins, particularly injustice (1:3-4, 6, 9, 11, 13, 2:1, 4). Israel is confronted for their abuse of the poor:

Thus says the LORD, "For three transgressions of Israel and for four I will not revoke its punishment, Because they sell the righteous for money And the needy for a pair of sandals. "These who pant after the very dust of the earth on the head of the helpless Also turn aside the way of the humble; And a man and his father resort to the same girl in order to profane My Holy Name. (Amos 2:6-7)

The profaning of the Name of God was tied to unjust acts (v.7). The law was bent toward those who could afford to bribe rulers—one law for the rich and another for the poor. Israel had erred in that the poor were being exploited by the wealthy, "sold for a pair of sandals (v.6)." In ancient Israel, the "gate" was the place justice was meted out between parties

(Deuteronomy 16:18; 17:8; 21:19; 25:7). In that culture as well as today, bribery was used to sway legal decisions in favor of those who could afford to pay. In that sense, the poor were at the mercy of those who could corrupt judges to rule in their favor.

The covenant people of God further corrupted themselves through sexual sin, which was even jointly shared between father and son (v.7). They collectively had lost a sense of shame for their sins. Unlike the man who appeared before the judge awaiting his punishment, they were clueless to their doom. The LORD God had sent His prophet Amos to call the nation to repent so they might be forgiven and restored instead of judged and punished.

Today, it is a well-known fact that those who can afford highly qualified legal representation will often fare better when tried in court. Some extremely wealthy criminals have been able to pay off accusers or even bribe witnesses to lessen their sentences or avoid punishment altogether. Well-documented disparities exist today within the American justice system. The Bureau of Justice Statistics and the United States Sentencing Commission notes that African American males receive weightier sentences and forms of judgment compared to their white counterparts.[19],[20] Even the ongoing shooting of unarmed black men and women has been a blight on the American justice system, provoking mass protests and even riots. It can seem that injustice is a common occurrence today as well as in ancient Israel, but is it right in the sight of God? And to what degree is the Christian to accept injustice or to stand against it?

Amos 5:21-24 records some of the strongest language used in the Bible. In these verses, God describes His view of worship devoid of justice toward others:

I hate, I despise your festivals, and I take no delight in your assemblies. Yes, even if you offer me your burnt offerings and

---

19   William Rhodes et al., "Federal Sentencing Disparity: 2005-2012," Bureau of Justice Statistics Working Papers Series.

20   William H. Pryor Jr. et al., "Demographic Differences in Sentencing: An Update to the 2012 Booker Report," United States Sentencing Commission.

grain offerings, I will not accept them, and I will not look at the fellowship offerings of your fattened animals. Remove from me the noise of your songs, and I do not want to hear the melody of your harps! But let justice roll on like the water, and righteousness like an ever-flowing stream.

God despised their religious festivals and refused to accept any offerings of repentance (burnt, grain, fellowship) or musical worship (vv.22-23). Instead, He commanded, "But let justice roll on like water, and righteousness like an ever-flowing stream" (v.24).

The Israelites were surrounded by opportunities to act with restorative justice for people who had been oppressed or treated unjustly in Israel. They also were to act retributively through the equitable rule of law. But sadly, they refused the call to repent, to mourn their wrongs, and to change their ways. In 722 BC, the Assyrian empire would sack, invade, and take Israel into exile. Part of what led to their downfall was their unwavering trust in ungodly leadership.

Amos prophesied during the reign of Jeroboam II. He was a contemporary of the prophet Jonah. But unlike Jonah, the prophecies Amos gave to Jeroboam II included judgment. In the preceding verses, Amos spoke of the hatred for hypocritical and false worship by God. Justice was to be concrete actions to restore the downtrodden or to contend against the wicked.

Justice is a theme repeated in the prophets: "Thus says the Lord, do justice and righteousness and deliver the one who has been robbed from the power of his oppressor. Also, do not mistreat or do violence to the stranger the orphan or the widow and do not shed innocent blood in this place" (Jeremiah 22:3). The most vulnerable were to receive restorative justice through the people of God. Repeatedly in Scripture, the Lord identified with the weak and the vulnerable (i.e., "Father to the Fatherless and Judge for widows" Psalm 68:5). You see Him taking up the plight of those the world exploits, abuses, and discards.

When the Israelites received the Law again as a new generation was preparing to enter the promised land, God reminded them of Himself. He related to them the covenant He made with the forefathers and their rescue from bondage in Egypt. It is important to note His view of justice toward the vulnerable among His covenant people and what He commands them to do in Deuteronomy 10:14-22:

> *Behold, to the LORD your God belong heaven and the highest heavens, the earth and all that is in it. "Yet on your fathers did the LORD set His affection to love them, and He chose their descendants after them, even you above all peoples, as it is this day. "So circumcise your heart, and stiffen your neck no longer. "For the LORD your God is the God of gods and the Lord of lords, the great, the mighty, and the awesome God who does not show partiality nor take a bribe. "He executes justice for the orphan and the widow, and shows His love for the alien by giving him food and clothing. "So show your love for the alien, for you were aliens in the land of Egypt. "You shall fear the LORD your God; you shall serve Him and cling to Him, and you shall swear by His name. "He is your praise and He is your God, who has done these great and awesome things for you which your eyes have seen. "Your fathers went down to Egypt seventy persons in all, and now the LORD your God has made you as numerous as the stars of heaven.*

God declared His Sovereign rule over heaven and earth; He also affirmed the unique love He set on Israel above all "people" (nations). But this was not to induce a sense of superiority, for God is not partial (v.17). Instead, He acts justly and does not take a bribe. Justice and love were to be a shield for orphans, widows, aliens, and strangers among Israel because of who God is and because Israel, too, were aliens in Egypt (v.19). Those most in need were also to receive retributive justice through opposing those who would mistreat or do violence to them. The character of God has not changed. His people must act justly, love mercy, and walk humbly with Him (Micah 6:8).

In the United States, matters of justice are hotly debated. Immigration policy has been fought over for decades. Recently, it has been televised that children entering the U.S. alone, with parents, or some adult illegally have been detained and placed in holding centers. It is egregious that children in legitimate family units have been separated from their parents. The government has authority (Romans 13) that should not intrude on the sphere of the Church or the sphere of the family. Based on Scripture, I cannot support leadership that affirms the separation of families. In James 1:27, true worship is equated to a right relationship with God ("keeping oneself unspotted from the world") and true compassion toward the most vulnerable ("to visit the fatherless and widow in their affliction").

The justice of God calls for humble recognition of our own sins (Luke 18:9-14). The Pharisees were guilty of false judgments and were guilty before God for their self-righteousness. When God judges sin, all are guilty before Him (Romans 3:23), and the punishment due is death (6:23) apart from the gift of God through faith in Jesus Christ (3:16). Chris Marshall from the Center for Christian ethics provides helpful insights on biblical justice:

> God's justice is retributive inasmuch as it is never prejudiced, arbitrary, or impulsive, and is always morally attuned to human deeds and deserts. Yet it focuses not on the imposition of retribution on wrongdoers, but the restoration of a right relationship.[21]

There is a sense that God can act providentially and through governments to punish evildoers (Romans 13:4; 1 Peter 2:14), which Marshall described. But more than that, God, through His justice, restores and reconciles man to God and God to man. When Christ brought Zacchaeus to repentance and faith, he exclaimed in Luke 19:8, "Behold, Lord, half of my possessions I will give to the poor, and if I have defrauded anyone of anything, I will give back four times as much." Salvation had come to Zacchaeus (v.9). Now as a follower of Christ, he sought to restore what he had taken unlawfully.

---

21 Chris Marshall, "Divine Justice as Restorative Justice," Center for Christian Ethics, 2012, pg. 15.

Fundamental to discussions about justice is an understanding that it is not about seeing all people as oppressed or oppressor but rather as sinful people who need the Lord and Savior Jesus Christ (Romans 3:23). From a sinful heart, injustice, slander, hatred, racism, and all evil arise (Matthew 15:19; Mark 7:21). The Christian must not condone racism or oppression by affirming injustice but instead must act justly (Micah 6:8).

The New Testament further commanded that masters were to "treat their slaves justly, knowing that you also have a Master in heaven" (Colossians 4:1). This passage alone has the power to end slavery and other forms of oppression. And everywhere true Christianity took root, people were changed through the gospel, and as a result, their lives and communities were transformed. These actions are a credible witness to the reality of a genuine relationship with Jesus Christ, like salt in a decaying world and light in darkness (Matthew 5:13-16). Injustice from the visible church defames the faith.

America has people from all over the world. In discussing racism, there tends to be a "black and white" only dialogue. Yet the American experience is rich in all cultures, including people of Asian descent. There are a variety of people with multiple languages, including Bangladesh, China, India, Indonesia, Japan, Korea, Malaysia, Myanmar, the Philippines, and Thailand. The U.S. has its own history of unethical laws related to immigrants from these places. During World War II, the Japanese were placed in internment camps based upon fear and anti-Asian or immigrant rhetoric.

At the writing of this book, some political leaders have termed the COVID-19 virus "the Chinese virus," or "the Chinese Flu." These comments have been highly insulting to many and have been associated with hate crimes toward not only people from China but other Asian backgrounds as well. Because all people are made in the image of God, we are commanded not to curse or kill people (Genesis 9:6; James 3:8-10). As laws are written and enforced, followers of Jesus Christ must contend with the "rightness" of those laws based upon the standard of justice and righteousness in His sight.

In matters of justice, the Christian is not to seek revenge against his enemy but must, instead, love him (Matthew 5:44). Vengeance belongs to God, who will repay (Romans 12:19). The Lord has also instructed Christians to seek the restoration of fellow Christians who fall into sin

(Galatians 6:1). For the unrepentant among the Christian community, we must repeatedly seek to confront sin in love with an admonishment to return and be restored (Matthew 18:15-20).

Even the parable of the unforgiving servant illustrates God's patience in seeking restorative justice for the repentant. As we close this section, one may wonder, *How can I act with justice and righteousness?* Through faith in Jesus Christ, we are empowered to love our neighbor and live under the law of Christ (Matthew 22:39; 1 Corinthians 9:21; Galatians 6:2). Through a relationship with Him, acting justly will seek to restore or defend others out of love.

PRAYER

"Father in heaven, thank you that your Rule is established upon justice and righteousness. We thank you that the greatest injustice that ever occurred was upon your Son, Our Lord Jesus Christ, who took the punishment for our sins in our place. Thank you for being just and the justifier of all men. Grant us to be your instruments of justice in righteousness, where we live as salt and light. Please help us to truly worship you and live justly, love mercy, and walk humbly with You. In the Name of Jesus Christ. Amen."

DISCUSSION QUESTIONS

1. Is the church obligated to practice justice only to herself? Yes or No? Why?
2. How do we view justice in light of the cross of Jesus Christ?
3. Who are the vulnerable among us and how should they receive justice?
4. What collections of Scriptures (Old and New Testaments) inform you of justice?
5. If Amos were to visit the church in America today, what would he say?

4 JOHN THE BAPTIST

God Commands Bearing Fruit Of Repentance

*D*eserts are known for their dry, harsh, merciless landscapes where extraordinarily little vegetation can live. The dryness and hardness of the soil make it difficult for plants to take root and for fruit to develop. The deadness of the earth is reflected in how little it produces. I knew a gentleman who worked on the power lines in the deserts of California. He was a rough man who had lived a hard life, and he was skeptical of anything from the Bible.

One day his sister invited him to a church picnic where a visiting evangelist shared a few words. Briefly, the minister welcomed everyone to the feast and illustrated that they were invited to another feast, but not all would enter (See the parable of the wedding feast – Matthew 22:1-14). As the preacher compelled them to turn from their sins and place their faith in Jesus Christ, the man became convinced that he needed the Lord Jesus Christ for forgiveness. That day marked a change in Him. He asked to receive Jesus Christ and began to pray and read the Bible for himself.

Little by little, as his faith grew, his demeanor changed. Genuine, not forced, changes were noticeable. He was happy. No longer did he walk around with a sour look but was sincerely happy. He began to invite his friends to church. Christ Jesus had so changed his heart that he would pick up senior citizens from nursing homes and drive them back and forth to church. On the day of his baptism, he shared humbly with everyone, "I thank God for forgiving me. I place my faith now in Jesus Christ, and I love everybody." The power of God to change a heart is miraculous—like changing a desert to a garden of fruit trees.

John the Baptist was a prophet of God sent to call Israel to repent. His message was a command for the people to "bear fruit in keeping with repentance" (Luke 3:8). The people were called to produce real change in their lives and not to depend on their national-ethnic identity (Matthew 3:9). True change can only come by grace through faith in Jesus Christ (Ephesians 2:8-10). He is the source for forgiveness and good works emanating from and motivated by Him. For the nation of Israel, it was a command to produce real fruit.

The Gospel of Luke is an accurate account of the events surrounding the life, death, and resurrection of Jesus Christ (1:1-4). John was the last prophet, preceding the coming of Jesus Christ. As a prophet, he received the Word of God (3:2). The message came during dark times, after years of silence from God toward Israel. The nation was ruled by exceedingly wicked political rulers (Tiberius Caesar, Pontius Pilate, Herod, Phillip, and Lysanias – 3:1). Tiberius Caesar, in his debauchery, wore animal skins and hunted children to ravish them on the Island of Capri (Suetonius, *The Lives of Twelve Caesars*, Life of Tiberius).

To make matters worse, the spiritual leaders of Israel, Annas and Caiaphas (father-in-law and son-in-law, 3:2), both shared the high priesthood and were Sadducees—a religious sect that did not believe in the resurrection or eternal life. They were spiritually bankrupt and could not lead Israel in returning to God. The nation of Israel was under godless and spiritually dead leadership, which drew them further away from God. The message that He gave through the voice of John was *repent!*

John the Baptist's call was to preach a baptism of repentance. His voice was that of a king's forerunner (Luke 3:4-5; Isaiah 40:3). Just as Isaiah prophesied before him as a "voice crying out in the wilderness, make ready the way of the Lord, make His paths straight," John called the nation to make ready for the coming Messiah (Anointed King), Jesus Christ. Forerunners in the ancient world ran before the king and his transport to clear roadways of debris and to fill up paths that had ravines. His call to repent and be baptized was also for gentiles and Jews.

Gentile proselytes engaged in a ceremony of baptism to convert to the Jewish faith. Apart from this act, they were considered unclean and were to be avoided. When Jews required cleansing from exposure to sin or ritual defilement before going to the Temple, they performed a ritual bathing (mikva) to be ceremonially clean before God. The call given in preparation for the coming of Jesus Christ was for all to repent and be baptized! Everyone in Israel needed divine cleansing! Divine cleansing is radically different from ceremonial cleansing. Only God alone can forgive sin (Mark 2:7). Jesus Christ highly affirmed John (7:28), and we would do well to consider His call to repentance.

> *So he began saying to the crowds who were going out to be baptized by him, "You brood of vipers, who warned you to flee from the wrath to come? _"Therefore bear fruits in keeping with repentance, and do not begin to say to yourselves, 'We have Abraham for our father,' for I say to you that from these stones God is able to raise up children to Abraham. _"Indeed the axe is already laid at the root of the trees; so every tree that does not bear good fruit is cut down and thrown into the fire." And the crowds were questioning him, saying, "Then what shall we do?" _ And he would answer and say to them, "The man who has two tunics is to share with him who has none; and he who has food is to do likewise." And some tax collectors also came to be baptized, and they said to him, "Teacher, what shall we do?" And he said to them, "Collect no more than what you have been ordered to." _Some soldiers were questioning him, saying, "And what about us, what shall we do?" And he said to them, "Do not take money from anyone by force, or accuse anyone falsely, and be content with your wages." (Luke 3:7-14)*

The message confronted their pride and sense of security and called for a demonstration of their faith if they were truly converted. They were called a "brood of vipers," (v.7) fleeing from the wrath of God like snakes fleeing a brush fire. Religion in Israel had become fake, routine, and hypocritical. They were warned by John not to seek security in their ethnic-national identity as "sons of Abraham." They thought being a "Jew" was enough for them to be considered in a right relationship with God, not realizing that destruction was nearer than they thought (i.e., the axe is laid at the root of the trees, v.9).

Not only Israel had these disastrous characteristics in its politicians, spiritual leaders, and people, but we, too, have it in America. At the writing of this book, we are amid a pandemic where, thus far, over 220,000 Americans have lost their lives to COVID-19. And the country is in the middle of some of the worst ethnic strife in nearly five decades. We, too, have ethnic-national pride: "I'm an American!" And sometimes we express a sense of elitism when compared to other nations when, in fact, God alone can bless or bring calamity upon nations who go against His will (Jeremiah 18:5-10).

God had moved upon the hearts of the people. They had asked John, "What shall we do? (v.10)? Those who had more than others could demonstrate their repentance by being generous with their material possessions (v.11). Tax collectors could demonstrate their repentance by showing integrity in their tax collection (vv.12-13), not taking more than required. And for soldiers, repentance meant breaking from the practices of extortion, false accusation, and flat-out robbery (v.14). Instead, soldiers were to be content with their pay.

Two observations concerning conversion and transformation can be seen in this section of Luke. First, only God can change the human heart. For a person to be truly changed, they must be born again (John 3:1-16). The audience heard the gospel of Jesus Christ through John and were moved by the Holy Spirit to repent and believe. Second, genuine faith will have works (Ephesians 2:8-10; James 2:14-26). Love for God and a real, living faith will bear fruits in righteous acts that are pleasing to Him. A person's very possessions and vocations can become a means for good works.

Those who have been given ample resources in this life, who formerly hoarded them, are now free to share them with love when they truly repent of their greed. And those who have dishonored Christ in their daily work can now love Him and others through it. Those who have been born again do not necessarily have to leave their vocations or completely abandon their belongings. Instead, they begin to serve Christ in that area of life.

In Acts 10-11 a Roman centurion named Cornelius received a vision from God. An angel told him God had heard his prayers and seen his gifts to the poor (10:1-4). Through the ministry of Peter, he heard the gospel, became born-again, and received the gift of the Holy Spirit (11:15-18). Interestingly, he remained a centurion. As a Roman military leader, he commanded legions of warriors who worked under the direction of Caesar. Yet in his vocation, he found opportunities to do good to the poor and maintain peace as a soldier. If repentance and faith change the spiritual state of a man, fruits of repentance will change the deeds of a man for good.

In discussing racism and ethnic strife, the subject of policing and law enforcement is strongly debated. Many are angered by the abuse of authority and unlawful use of force in the death of ethnic minorities. Others feel that law enforcement is being unfairly blamed and have an increasingly thankless job as those who serve and protect the community. Based on John's message, everyone needs repentance and faith, including law enforcement.

Godly law enforcement, like any other vocation, is needed. It is made up of individuals who need to place their faith in Jesus Christ. Those who may be tempted to or have extorted, harassed, or illegitimately threatened the lives of people also need to repent. Those who have worn the mantle well should be honored and respected. Governments and ruling authorities are ultimately established by God and should be respected (Romans 13), yet they too are accountable to Him.

Scripture records that when Nebuchadnezzar boasted that he made Babylon great, God struck him with insanity until he recognized that the Most High God rules (Daniel 4). Amazingly, God brought him to repentance and Nebuchadnezzar honored and exalted God, who can humble those who walk in pride (vv.36-37). When the Apostle Paul wrote the Ephesian church, he reminded masters (those who rule others) of their status before God: "And masters, do the same things to them, and give up threatening, knowing that both their Master and yours is in heaven, and there is no partiality with Him" (Ephesians 6:9).

Those who were to imitate Christ as masters were to be servants and not despots, knowing that only God ruled over all. The very authority wielded by mankind is done as a manager of the resources and abilities God has provided for His purposes (1 Corinthians 4:1). All people are accountable before God and commanded to repent, including leaders.

When the message of repentance reached Herod, he wickedly imprisoned John.

> So with many other exhortations he preached the gospel to the people. But when Herod the tetrarch was reprimanded by him because of Herodias, his brother's wife, and because of all the wicked things which Herod had done, Herod also added this to them all: he locked John up in prison.

John preached the gospel of Jesus Christ. During his ministry, he confronted the wickedness of Herod, who had taken his brother's wife, Herodias. It was an immoral act for anyone, but particularly for a ruler of Israel. Later, out of spite, Herodias prompted her daughter Salome to ask for the head of John the Baptist after she enticed Herod with her dance (Matthew 14:6; Mark 6:17-22). Herod later paid for his pride when the people praised him, saying, "Voice of a God!" Since he did not give God the glory, he was struck by God with worms and died (Acts 12:21-23). The horror of an unconverted life is seen in its consequences.

When people receive the gospel and their lives are converted to Christ, He will bring about a change that will glorify Him in that culture. Proverbs 14:34 says, "Righteousness exalts a nation, but sin is a reproach to any people." Some people hold their faith as a private matter. But fruits of repentance are outward evidences, not contrived but an outgrowth of an inward reality.

A sad commentary on the church in America is that it often conveys the same values and actions of those who deny the faith. Churches often assemble along the same political party lines (Democratic and Republican). And their constituencies will capitulate to the values of those groups even when they disagree with biblical doctrine and are slow to confront the sinfulness of its leaders in the manner of John the Baptist. Although some will speak out against these practices, often the Sunday gatherings are an indictment on the spiritual decay of the American church into a political-ethnic tribe rather than a house of prayer for all the nations (Mark 11:17).

The American church agrees that racism is a sin that divides the people of God illegitimately. Therefore, why is there so little "fruit of repentance" in this area on Sunday? Few churches (even within their own denominations) reflect the ethnic makeup of their communities. Bearing fruit might include turning to our neighbors with the gospel and seeking them rather than avoiding them.

For one man from Southern California, change had come! He was happy. He received Jesus Christ and was forgiven. He had peace with God and with his neighbors. He was free to love and be loved and single-handedly brought anyone to church who was interested. But even more so, as a member of the body of Christ, He brought the gospel to others. This was no gimmick, hype, or sense of grandstanding. It was joy! It was refreshing to see God bring about fruits of repentance in one man in a little church. Just as an oasis in the desert is a drastic change of scenery, this man had a change of heart.

PRAYER

"We give you thanks, Heavenly Father, through sending your Word to call all people to repent. Thank you for the opportunity to turn from our sins and their evils to turn to you who love us and gave your only Son, Jesus Christ. Be pleased to produce eternal change in our hearts and lives. May we bear fruit to your honor and praise. Amen."

DISCUSSION QUESTIONS

1. How did God use John the Baptist to prepare the Israelites for the coming of Christ?
2. How are Christians called to prepare people for the coming of Jesus Christ?
3. What are "fruits of repentance?"

4. Can fruits of repentance be evidence of genuine repentance and faith?

5. When a person comes to faith in Christ, how will it affect their life vocation and worldview?

5 PEOPLE FROM EVERY TRIBE, TONGUE, AND NATION

*J*t is an honor to serve people as a chaplain in their moments before dying. The sense of urgency, seriousness, and solemnity of those moments are unforgettable. One man who faced death with his wife recited the 23rd Psalm as he breathed his last breath with the quiet assurance that Jesus Christ had forgiven his sins. Another person kissed each family member goodbye, praying for each one and sending each one off so she might meet with God on her own. Another sat down and asked me to write a letter asking for forgiveness from his estranged daughter and offering her forgiveness as well, expressing love and peace with God and with her. Our times are in His hands (Psalm 31:15). In those moments, issues such as racism seem so small, particularly in light of the plan of God for all eternity.

In the book of Revelation, the prophecy was given to the Apostle John of the "things which must soon take place" (Revelation 1:1). The book contains the following outline:

- Chapter 1– Introduction and greetings
- Chapters 2-3 – Messages to the seven churches
- Chapters 4-5 – Prelude scene in heaven
- Chapters 6-16 – Seal, trumpet, and bowl Judgments unleashed
- Chapters 17-18 – The fall of Babylon
- Chapters 19-21 – The return of Jesus Christ, the Millennium, and the new heaven and new earth

In the early chapters of Revelation, a heavenly scene unfolds where the Lord Jesus Christ is described as the "Lamb." This title is repeated throughout the book. As judgment will occur on the earth, only one is fit and worthy to open the seals of God to begin this momentous event. Revelation 5:8-10 reads:

When He had taken the book, the four living creatures and the twenty-four elders fell down before the Lamb, each one holding a harp and golden bowls full of incense, which are the prayers of the saints. And they sang a new song, saying, "Worthy are You to take the book and to break its seals; for You were slain, and purchased for God with Your blood men from every tribe and tongue and people and nation. You have made them to be a kingdom and priests to our God; and they will reign upon the earth."

The Apostle John received a glorious vision of heaven. In this scene, Jesus Christ appeared and was honored around the throne for His wonderful, sacrificial work. He is the Lamb who was slain. The Jewish sacrificial system involved the slaying of lambs to make atonement for sins (Romans 9:22). Isaiah 53 would direct the ancient Jew to the Suffering Servant of the LORD, the Messiah, and His greater sacrifice that would "sprinkle the nations" with His own blood (52:15). When John the Baptist saw Jesus Christ approaching to be baptized, he hailed, "Behold, the Lamb of God that takes away the sins of the world" (John 1:29). In this vision of heaven in Revelation 5:8-10, Jesus Christ is hailed for having purchased with His blood men from every tribe, tongue, people, and nation.

Every "tribe" (v.9) represents descendants of people paid for with the blood of Jesus Christ. Like descendants of Abraham, Christ had laid claim to different people within various tribes—each one bought by Him. People from differing "tongues," commonly called languages, are among the elect. And "people" may refer to the people of God among Israel and/or the Church. "Nation" or ethnos speaks of the foreigner, the people not near but from afar. These groups that once were separated by these earthly divisions are consumed by the awesome Lamb.

It is important to consider what the plan of God is for the nations when discussing ethnic hatred, prejudice, and racism. From the beginning, God made us in His image to represent Him throughout the world (Genesis 1:26-28). Nations were made by God (Acts 17:26). When mankind rebelled against God's command to "fill the earth" and assembled on the plains of Shinar to build a tower into the heavens (Babel), God confused their speech (Genesis 11). Their motive was to make a "name for themselves" and not to be "scattered" (Genesis 11:4).

God instead executed His plan to bless the nations through one man, named Abraham. The LORD promised to "make his name great," "bless those who bless," "curse those who curse," and in Abraham, "all the families of the earth" would be blessed (Genesis 12:1-4). Where mankind seeks to be great and be like God (3:5; 11:4), God chose to specifically make one man great and to bless the world through him. Ultimately, this promise is fulfilled in Jesus Christ— the Son of Abraham, Son of David, and Son of God.

This Abrahamic covenant is the backdrop to the stage of world events. God Himself, through Jesus Christ, is reaching, redeeming, and equipping His saints among the nations to be a kingdom to Himself. Once separated by language at Babel (Genesis 11), now completely united eternally in worship to God.

The history of the Old and New Testaments bear witness to the kingdom of God reaching people from among all nations. Rahab was brought among the people of Israel through her role in hiding Israelite spies in Jericho (Joshua 2; James 2:25). Ruth the Moabitess left her country to cleave to Naomi and the God of Israel (Ruth 1-4). Naaman the Syrian commander, through his healing, came to faith in the LORD God (2 Kings 5). An Ethiopian Eunuch received Christ and baptism through the teaching of Phillip (Acts 8:26-40). Cornelius the Roman centurion received Christ and the gift of the Holy Spirit, along with his household (Acts 10).

Ancient, modern, and contemporary church history is full of stories where the truth concerning the Lord Jesus Christ has been preached from person to person—spanning culture to culture. Missionaries have traveled globally, and ordinary Christians have reached others locally. Some examples have been Saint Patrick and his missionary work in Ireland;[22] Frumentius and Edesius, taking the gospel of Jesus Christ to the rulers of the Axumite empire of Africa;[23] Boniface and his mission within Germany;[24] Elizabeth Elliot and her husband Jim Elliot to the Auca Indians;[25] and the daily quiet devotion of men and women within the nation who choose to step outside of their comfort zone to compel people to be reconciled to Christ.

As the prophecy of Revelation unfolds, the events concerning the kingdom rule of Christ over all nations are true. All peoples will worship, and those who desire to obey the great commission (Matthew 28:16-20) may experience a glimpse of what eternal worship will be. It has been said by the late Rev. Martin Luther King Jr. that Sunday at 11 a.m. is the most segregated hour in America. This is not the case among the elect of God, redeemed by the blood of Jesus Christ for eternity. In the face of continued and growing ethnic hatred and racial tension, it takes courage for Christian churches to pursue all people with the gospel of Jesus Christ. It is easy to retreat to the ethnic, cultural, and social group that is most familiar instead of advancing to make disciples from among the nations.

Just as the lesson of Jonah revealed God as compassionate, gracious, slow to anger, and abounding in mercy (Exodus 34:6-7; Jonah 4:2), people need to turn to Him in repentance and faith while there is still time. The truth of the gospel compels us to make this message known to all men because it is appointed unto all men to die and then after that, the judgment (Hebrews 9:27). This sobering reality should motivate Christians. A biblical

---

22   Saint Patrick, "The Confession of Saint Patrick," (N.p., CreateSpace Independent Publishing Platform, 2013), 9.

23   Elizabeth Isichei, *A History of Christianity in Africa: From Antiquity to the Present*, (United States, Eerdmans Publishing Company, 1995), 32-33.

24   John Foxe, *Book of Martyrs: A Universal History of Christian Martyrdom*, (United States, Key, Mielke & Biddle, 1832), 4.

25   Elisabeth Elliot, *Through Gates of Splendor: The Event that Shocked the World, Changed a People, and Inspired a Nation*, (United States, Hendrickson Publishers Marketing, 2010).

response to what divides us includes remembering the truth that all people will give an account to God. He requires justice and righteousness from all people, not only in the days of Amos but today. Because all men sin and fall short of the glory of God (Romans 3:23), we need a Savior from the judgment rightfully due (6:23). True change will occur, and last, with fruits of repentance that will evidence changed lives (Luke 3).

Those who reject Christ Jesus and choose to go their own way will find themselves standing before God carrying their own sins and their name not found in the Lamb's book of life among the redeemed (Revelation 20:11-15; 21:27), then departing into the lake of fire (20:15). But because of the great love of God, there is hope for the reader. Christ died and rose on behalf of sinners so that those who repent and believe in Him would have eternal life (John 3:16; 1 Corinthians 15:3-4; 2 Corinthians 5:21). May all who truly believe in the Lord Jesus Christ strive to make disciples from among all the nations by His grace (Matthew 28:16-20; 1 Corinthians 15:10).

In a far better world, where there is a new heaven and earth, all sin, sorrow, and death will be removed (Revelation 21:1-5). The Lord God Almighty and the Lamb will make all things new and bring light to His redeemed nations (vv.22-27). In that place, a river of the water of life, coming from the throne of God Himself, will have trees of life on either side, bearing fruit for the healing of the nations (22:1-2). No longer divided by sin but united eternally with Him.

PRAYER

"Father in heaven, thank you for sending Jesus Christ to rescue us from our sins and return us to you. Thank you, Christ Jesus, for preparing a place for us in your eternal kingdom where we may worship you as the Lamb. To you be all glory, honor, and praise for purchasing by your blood people from every tribe, tongue, and nation. In your Holy Name. Amen"

DISCUSSION QUESTIONS

1. Who are the people from every tribe, tongue (language), and nation in Revelation 5:9?

2. What hinders worship across ethnic groups today?

3. How has unresolved ethnic strife inhibited Christian worship among the nations?

4. Where in Scripture are glimpses of the power of God to unite people of different ethnic backgrounds?

5. When a person becomes regenerate, do they lose their ethnic identity presently? Eternally?

6. Why is it difficult for professing Christians of different ethnic backgrounds to worship together?

7. What Scriptures describe the history of Jew and gentile worship in the Bible?

BIBLIOGRAPHY

Dabney, Robert Lewis. *A Defence of Virginia: (and Through Her, of the South) in Recent and Pending Contests Against the Sectional Party*. United States: E.J. Hale, 1867.

Dabney, Robert Lewis. On Secular Education. Russia: Canon Press, 1996.

Darwin, Charles. *On the Origin of Species by Means of Natural Selection, Or, The Preservation of Favoured Races in the Struggle for Life*. United Kingdom: G. Richards, 1902.

Elliot, Elisabeth. *Through Gates of Splendor: The Event that Shocked the World, Changed a People, and Inspired a Nation*. United States: Hendrickson Publishers Marketing, 2010.

Foxe, John. *Book of Martyrs: A Universal History of Christian Martyrdom*. United States: Key, Mielke & Biddle, 1832.

Isichei, Elizabeth. *A History of Christianity in Africa: From Antiquity to the Present*. United States: Eerdmans Publishing Company, 1995.

MacArthur, John, and Richard Mayhue. *Biblical Doctrine: A Systematic Summary of Bible Truth*. Wheaton, IL: Crossway, 2017.

Mackie, T., and Collins, J. et al. "Bible Overviews: Old Testament: Jonah." The Bible Project. Accessed July 2020. https://bibleproject.com/all-videos/read-scripture-old-testament/.

Marshall, Chris. Divine Justice as Restorative Justice. Center for Christian Ethics, 2012.

Patrick, Saint. *The Confession of Saint Patrick*. N.p.: CreateSpace Independent Publishing Platform, 2013.

Piper, John. "Racial Harmony and Interracial Marriage." Desiring God. January 16, 2020. https://www.desiringgod.org/messages/racial-harmony-and-interracial-marriage.

Pryor Jr., William H. et al. "Demographic Differences in Sentencing: An Update to the 2012 Booker Report." United States Sentencing Commission.

Rhodes, William et al. "Federal Sentencing Disparity: 2005–2012." Bureau of Justice Statistics Working Papers Series.

Rushdoony, Rousas John, and North, Gary. *The Institutes of Biblical Law*. United States: Presbyterian and Reformed Publishing Company, 1973.

Rushdoony, Rousas John. *The Biblical Philosophy of History*. United States: Ross House Books, 2000.

Sanger, M., and Perry, M.W. and Wells, H.G. *The Pivot of Civilization in Historical Perspective: The Birth Control Classic*. Inkling Books, 2003.

Sanger, M. "The Eugenic Value of Birth Control Propaganda." *Birth Control Review* (October 1921): 5.

Sanger, M. Commenting on the 'Negro Project' in a letter to Dr. Clarence Gamble, December 10, 1939. – Sanger manuscripts, Sophia Smith Collection, Smith College, North Hampton, Massachusetts. Also described in Linda Gordon's *Woman's Body, Woman's Right: A Social History of Birth Control in America*. New York: Grossman Publishers, 1976.

Schwertley, Brian. "The Kinist Heresy: A Biblical Critique of Racism." Accessed August 21, 2020. http://www.reformedonline.com/uploads/1/5/0/3/15030584/kinist_heresy.pdf.

Spurgeon, Charles Haddon. "Separating the Precious from the Vile." *The New Park Street Pulpit*, vol. 6. Grand Rapids: Baker, 1994.

Suetonius, *The Twelve Caesars*. United Kingdom: Penguin, 2003.

APPENDIX A

Sermon Outlines

GENESIS 1:26-28, 9:6; COLOSSIANS 1:15-17; JAMES 3:9-12

THE IMAGE OF GOD: HIS FINGERPRINTS ON HIS CREATION

I. MADE IN HIS IMAGE (GENESIS 1:26A)

II. MADE IN HIS LIKENESS (GENESIS 1:26B)

    a. HUMANKIND, MALE AND FEMALE (GENESIS 1:27-28)

        I. TO BE FRUITFUL AND MULTIPLY

        II. TO SUBDUE IT AND RULE OVER IT

III. WARNING AGAINST KILLING THE IMAGE OF GOD (MURDER, 9:6)

IV. WARNING AGAINST CURSING THE IMAGE OF GOD (JAMES 3:9-12)

V. JESUS CHRIST IS THE IMAGE OF THE INVISIBLE GOD (COLOSSIANS 1:15-17)

JONAH 4:1-4, MATTHEW 12:41

JONAH: GOD'S COMPASSION IS DIFFERENT FROM OURS

I. JONAH REBELS AND RUNS FROM GOD (1:1-3, 7, 17)

    a. GOD SUPERNATURALLY PURSUES JONAH (VV.3-9)

    b. SAILORS REPENT, AND GOD RELENTS (VV.5-16)

II. JONAH PRAYS AND RECOMMITS (2:1-10)

III. JONAH PREACHED, AND NINEVEH REPENTS (3:1-10)

IV. JONAH CHOOSES DEATH OVER COMPASSION (4:1-4)

V. GOD TEACHES JONAH TRUE COMPASSION (4:5-11)

VI. JESUS CHRIST IS GREATER THAN JONAH (MATTHEW 12:41)

<u>AMOS 5:21-24, JEREMIAH 22:3, MICAH 6:8, 1 PETER 3:18</u>

AMOS: JUSTICE AND RIGHTEOUSNESS MATTER TO GOD

I. WHAT GOD HATES (5:21-23)
- a. HYPOCRITICAL & FALSE WORSHIP
  - i. FESTIVALS
  - ii. ASSEMBLIES
- c. INSINCERE REPENTANCE & GIVING
  - i. BURNT OFFERINGS
  - ii. GRAIN OFFERINGS
  - iii. PEACE OFFERINGS

II. WHAT GOD APPROVES (V.24)
- a. JUSTICE BETWEEN MAN AND MAN
- b. EVER FLOWING RIGHTEOUSNESS

III. JESUS CHRIST – THE JUST FOR THE UNJUST – 1 PETER 3:18

<u>LUKE 3:1-20, 7:18-30</u>

JOHN THE BAPTIST: BEAR FRUITS OF REPENTANCE

I. THE CALL OF THE PROPHET (3:1,2)

II. THE CONTENT OF THE GOSPEL HE PREACHED (vv.3-9)

III. THE RESPONSE CAUSED BY THE GOSPEL MESSAGE (vv. 10-14)

IV. THE CHARACTER OF THE PROPHET (15-17)

V. THE COMMITMENT TO CHRIST OF THE PROPHET AND THE REPENTANT (vv.18-20)

REVELATION 5:1-10

PEOPLE FROM EVERY TRIBE, TONGUE, PEOPLE, AND NATION WORSHIPPING THE LAMB

I. THE LAMB ALONE CAN OPEN THE BOOK OF THE SEVEN SEALS (vv.1-4)

II. THE LAMB HAS AUTHORITY TO JUDGE (vv.5-7)
- a. HE IS THE LION OF JUDAH (v.5)
- b. HE IS THE ROOT OF DAVID (v.5)
- c. HE HAS OVERCOME TO OPEN THE BOOK (v.5)
- d. HE HAS RECEIVED AUTHORITY FROM THE FATHER (v.7)

V. THE LAMB IS WORTHY (vv.8-10)
- a. WORSHIP FROM ANGELS AND ELDERS (v.8, 11-14)
- b. WORSHIP FROM ALL PEOPLES AND RULE OVER ALL PEOPLES (v.9-10)

APPENDIX B

Genocide Historical Dates

The following historical timeline is a list of genocides linked to a false view of the origins of mankind (anthropology). Whenever any people are not recognized as made in the image of God, it leads to unspeakable acts of evil. Repeatedly, one nation or people did not see the other as image-bearers and sought to justify horrendous acts. A sample of some historical genocides, which do not fully describe their extent, are as follows:

- Native American Genocide, 1492
- The Transatlantic Slave Trade, 16th–19th Century
- Dzungar Mongols, 1750
- The Indian Removal, 1830s
- The Circassian Genocide, 1872
- The Armenian Genocide, 1915–1917
- Holodomor, 1931–1933
- The Holocaust, 1941–1945
- The Indonesian Genocide, 1965–1966
- The Bangladesh Genocide, 1971
- The Cambodian Genocide, 1975–1979
- The Guatemalan Genocide, 1981–1983
- The Rwandan Genocide, 1994
- The Bosnian Genocide, 1992–1995
- Isil Genocides, 2014
- The Rohingya Genocide, 2017

CPSIA information can be obtained
at www.ICGtesting.com
Printed in the USA
FSHW011949200921
84898FS

9 781951 304362